The
Connell Short Guide
to
Angela Carter's

The Bloody Chamber

by
Erica Wagner

Contents

NOTES

A summary of the stories

The Bloody Chamber is a concise collection of ten stories of varying length. The first story, "The Bloody Chamber", is much longer than any of the others and sets the tone of the book. All the stories use themes and ideas from what are usually called "fairy tales", but with them create something completely new and original.

THE BLOODY CHAMBER

The Bloody Chamber is a version of the story of Bluebeard, made famous by the French writer Charles Perrault at the end of the 17th century. It also has similarities to a story usually called The Robber Bridegroom, which appeared in the fairy tales published in Germany by Jacob and Wilhelm Grimm at the beginning of the 19th century. The Bloody Chamber's nameless narrator is a poor girl whose father, a soldier, died when she was little; she has been raised by her "indomitable" mother. The story opens at night, on a train from Paris; our heroine has just married a very rich man who is taking her, on their wedding night, to his great estate in the north of France. This estate is on an island with a causeway which is periodically covered by the tides; the place bears a clear resemblance to Mont St Michel, in Normandy. We learn that our young heroine (she is just 17) was a student of piano at the Paris Conservatoire; she met her much older husband-to-be when she was hired to play in a grand salon. Her mother had doubts about the marriage because her suitor (who is also never named, but called only "the Marquis") had been married three times already: to a Romanian countess; to a famous artist's model; and to an opera singer. All of them met untimely deaths – the countess died in a boating accident just three months before our narrator's marriage. But she is enthralled by his wealth and his sinister charm and they are wed in a small ceremony in Paris.

When they arrive at the "faery solitude" of the castle she is introduced to a life of grandeur such as she has not known before, where her every wish can be answered by an army of servants. He takes her to bed, but not before she has discovered, in his great library, a cache of violent pornography. She is able to have a brief telephone conversation with her mother, telling her – not very convincingly – that she is happy in her new home.

That very night her husband receives a phone call from his agent, calling him on urgent business to New York – the young bride will be abandoned on her honeymoon. (The telephone, along with other clues such as styles of dress, place this story roughly during the Belle Époque, the period from the late 19th century until the start of the First

World War.) Before he leaves, however, he entrusts her with a set of keys to all the rooms in the castle, telling her that it is only the key to his "private study" that she must not use. And because the sea air affects the castle's pianos, he also hires a piano tuner, the blind son of the local blacksmith called Jean-Yves, to keep his bride's instruments playable.

When he leaves, she is bored; because there are so many servants, she has nothing to do. And so she goes, of course, to his "private study" – which turns out to be a torture chamber, the "bloody chamber" of the title, and the dreadful grave of his three past wives. The Romanian countess has been killed by the spikes of an iron maiden – and her blood stains the little key to the chamber and cannot be wiped away. In terror, she confides what she has discovered to Jean-Yves, who reveals that the locals call this place "the Castle of Murder".

And then, to her horror, her husband returns; explaining that he did not, in fact, have to go to New York, he asks for his keys. When she returns them he sees the stain on the key and her transgression is revealed; he presses it into her forehead, and it leaves a red mark that cannot be washed away. He tells her he is going to kill her, and that she should wash and dress herself and prepare for death in the bloody chamber. He tells her he will decapitate her. All the phone lines have gone dead; she cannot call for help. Jean-Yves offers her the comfort of his love, but still she must go, and bend her neck for her husband's sword. But just before the dreadful deed is done, her mother – who had suspected from the phone call that all was not well – comes storming into the room, having travelled from Paris to rescue her daughter. She shoots the Marquis dead; his bride inherits his estate but gives much of her wealth away, as it is so tainted. She and her mother, along with Jean-Yves, go back to Paris and open a music school; the mark on her forehead never goes away, but her blind husband cannot see it.

THE COURTSHIP OF MR LYON

The Courtship of Mr Lyon works off ideas from Beauty and the Beast, which first appeared in the form we know it in France, in the 18th century. Again we are in a world where cars and telephones exist, but which still registers as old-fashioned. A girl waits at home, in winter, for her father, who is driving home; but his car has stuck fast in the snow. He is out of petrol – he is dead broke, as a meeting with his lawyers has just told him.

But he has broken down outside a beautiful manor house with wrought iron gates; when he enters them they close behind him. No human being welcomes him, however, only a little dog – which leads him into the house, where there is food and drink and a telephone to call the local garage to repair his car – the bill, says the mechanic, to be paid by his invisible host. All is well until, on leaving, he plucks a rose, growing magically in the snow, for his daughter, Beauty, waiting at home. Then his host, angry at having been stolen from, appears and insists he bring his daughter back to the house. This is the Beast, who looks like a lion but speaks like a man.

Beauty comes to the house with trepidation; but the Beast treats her kindly – while he restores her father's fortunes too. So Beauty asks to visit her father, promising she will return to the Beast "before the winter is over".

She goes to London – to a glittering life of wealth, and forgets about the Beast. Spring is about to arrive. One evening she hears a scrabbling of claws outside her door: it is the little dog who greeted her father, but now matted and thin, frantic to bring her back to the Beast. Beauty knows that Beast is dying and hurries back to Beast's house with the little dog.

When she returns she finds him in a little plain attic room; he tells her he is dying. She falls upon him, weeping, kissing him and begging him not to die – where upon he is transformed into a handsome man – and the two of them live in the house with the little dog.

THE TIGER'S BRIDE

The Tiger's Bride is a different spin on the same story of Beauty and the Beast. This time the narrator is a young woman travelling from Russia with her father, a nobleman, who has squandered his fortune and now, arriving in a country described only as being in the south, wagers his daughter on a game of cards with "La Bestia", the Beast. The Beast in this story looks like a man but only because he is in a man's costume: he wears a long coat and gloves and a human mask. He cannot speak intelligibly; his valet speaks for him.

Her father loses the card game – and the narrator is taken away in the Beast's carriage to his decaying palazzo, all the while recalling stories told to her by her nursemaid about a "tiger-man" once seen in London. On arrival, the valet informs her that the Beast has only one desire: and that is to see her naked. She refuses. She is given a room, almost a cell, and a servant – who is not human, but an automaton replica of herself.

The Beast takes her hunting with him on horseback, knowing she will not run away because she is "a woman of honour". They ride to the riverside – where the Beast takes off his cloaking garments and reveals himself to be a tiger. Awed by the sight of him, she finally does as he asks, and stands naked before him. When they return to the house she is brought to a much finer, more opulent room – and she is told that she will be allowed to leave. Instead, however, she goes to see the Beast, who waits for her as his tiger-self, and when she arrives begins to lick her all over – and it seems as if she is being transformed into a tiger, too.

PUSS-IN-BOOTS

Puss-in-Boots is another story first found in a version by Charles Perrault; Carter's is high comedy, its narrator an Italianate ginger tomcat who is a loyal servant to his libidinous master. A cat – even one in boots – is easily able to slip into the bedrooms of young girls to bring them love notes and the like, so he is very useful. And then his master falls not in lust, but in love – with a woman who, unlike all the others, is kept highly guarded. She is the beautiful wife of an old man, Signor Panteleone, who ensures an old hag is always at her side to watch her; she is only allowed from the house to go to Mass, where Puss's master sits behind her in a pew and pines.

So Puss, with his own companion – a clever tabby cat – hatches a plot in which his master will disguise himself as a rat-catcher; the tabby will plant the rats in the lady's boudoir. The plan works – and the young man and his lady fall into each other's arms and make passionate love – and he is paid 100 ducats for his "rat- catching" services by

the hag! But he is resolved to live with her forever
– and so one morning the tabby cat slides under
the old husband's foot as he leaves for his office,
causing him to fall and break his neck; now the
young man poses as a doctor and pronounces him
dead. The old hag thinks something is amiss – but
a purse of gold keeps her quiet, as does the fact that
she's given money in Panteleone's will. And so the
young man and the new widow are married and
live happily – as do Puss-in-Boots and his tabby cat.

THE ERL-KING

The Erl-King is a title most associated with the
German poet Johann Wolfgang von Goethe; his
famous poem, *Erlkönig*, appeared in 1782 and was
famously set to music by Franz Schubert in 1815.
Carter's story, which has a dreamlike quality, is
narrated by an unnamed girl who goes into the
wood despite her knowledge that "Erl-King will do
you grievous harm". As she tells her story she
moves between first person, second person ("you")
and third person techniques.

It seems she goes to find him: his "bird-haunted
solitude", his house and garden in the middle of the
forest, are described in great detail. When she is
there Erl-King strips her naked and they become
lovers, though their love-making is elliptically
described. A violin without strings hangs in Erl-

King's house, soundlessly; at the end of the story he lays his head in her lap; she combs out his hair – and then strangles him. She frees his caged birds and they transform into the women they were before Erl-King captured them; with his hair she strings the violin, and it plays without a hand touching it.

THE SNOW CHILD

The Snow Child is the shortest story in the book. Its opening bears similarities to the opening of the Grimms' story, Snow White, in which a queen hopes for a child as red as blood, as white as snow and black as wood; but otherwise it is very different. In this story a Count and a Countess are riding in winter, and the Count wishes aloud for a girl as white as snow, as red as a hole filled with blood and black as a raven; she appears before him as he speaks, naked.

The Count puts her on the front of his saddle; the Countess is jealous, and drops her glove in the snow, ordering the girl to pick it up. The Count won't allow it; the Countess's rich furs spring from her shoulders to clothe the girl. The same thing happens with the Countess's diamond brooch – so the Countess is naked and the girl is clothed. But when the Countess asks for a rose, he allows the girl to pick it. She catches her finger on a thorn –

and dies. The Count has sex with the dead girl's body and it melts away; the Countess's clothes return to her body. The Count hands her the rose the Snow Child picked; it pricks the Countess as he hands it to her.

THE LADY OF THE HOUSE OF LOVE

The Lady of the House of Love belongs to the genre of vampire literature, which had its roots in the 18th century; the most famous example is Bram Stoker's *Dracula* (1897). In this story, narrated in the third person, the queen of the vampires, "Countess Nosferatu", sits alone in her castle, a victim of her appetites – which she despises. "Her beauty is a symptom of her disorder." She turns her pack of Tarot cards over and over, and they always show the same: La Papesse (The High Priestess), La Mort (Death) and La Tour Abolie (The Tower). On moonless nights she goes into the garden, heavily scented with roses, and catches small animals and sucks their blood. During the day she lies in her coffin. Sometimes local boys and men come to the fountain outside her house to wash; she leads them to her bedroom and kills them. Her governess disposes of their clothes and bones.

Then a young officer in the British Army, on a

holiday tour of the Carpathian mountains, comes near her castle. The time is revealed to be just before the start of the First World War; he is travelling by bicycle, "the most rational mode of transport in the world". Like the local boys and men, he washes the dust of his travels off in the fountain, and is brought into the castle by the governess and led to the countess.

Something about the young soldier unnerves her; she drops her Tarot cards; when he stoops to help gather them, the card of The Lovers is revealed. He thinks she is strange and sick but beautiful; she wears dark glasses to protect her eyes from the light. When she leads him into her chamber she drops her dark glasses and they break; gathering the pieces she cuts her hand and bleeds. The soldier kisses the wound – and then knows nothing more until he awakes in the light, and sees her dead in her boudoir, sitting up at the table. He leaves the castle, and is presumably safe – but when he returns to his regiment, he smells the scent of Nosferatu's roses in the barracks; and the next day is sent, along with his fellow soldiers, to the front in France.

THE WEREWOLF

The Werewolf is the first of three lycanthropic tales that finish the volume; this one, like the one that follows, The Company of Wolves, spins off from Little Red Riding Hood, another story from Charles Perrault. Here, in a "northern country", a third-person narration tells us of a little girl sent into the woods with a basket for her grandmother; she carries her father's hunting knife for protection. As she moves through the forest, she encounters a terrible wolf, which attacks her – she is brave, however, and strikes back, cutting off its paw. She wraps the paw in a cloth and puts it in her basket.

When she gets to her grandmother's house, she finds her sick in bed, delirious with fever. She goes to take the cloth the paw is wrapped in to make a cold compress for her grandmother's forehead – but discovers that the paw has turned into a human hand: her grandmother's hand. She pulls back the covers to reveal the bloody stump; her shrieking brings the neighbours who chase the grandmother out of the house and stone her to death. The little girl, we are told, now lives in the grandmother's house: "she prospered".

THE COMPANY OF WOLVES

The Company of Wolves is also set in a region of mountains and forests; it is winter. The beginning of the story is a series of werewolf legends that people speak of in this country; and then, the story itself begins with another brave girl heading into

the woods to see her grandmother. She too carries
a knife, and hears the howl of a wolf: but it is a
handsome young man who springs up before her
on the path. He charms her, and shows her his
compass; he challenges her to a race to her
grandmother's house, he through the forest, she on
the path. If she loses, she will have to give him a
kiss; she agrees, and hopes to lose.

He gets there first – and becomes his wolf-self,
devouring the grandmother, disposing of hair and
bones in the fire. He smooths out her bed, puts her
Bible on the table beside the bed, and waits for the
girl. When she arrives, she sees her grandmother
has gone – and when she sees a tuft of white hair in
the fire, knows she will die too. Wolves howl
outside. The wolf tells her to undress, but it is the
girl who instigates the undressing; when she stands
naked before him she steps into his arms, and he
lays his head on her lap so she can pick the lice
from his fur. The end of the story finds her sleeping
in her grandmother's bed, "between the paws of
the tender wolf".

WOLF-ALICE

Wolf-Alice is the story of a girl who was found in a
wolf's den, by the bullet-riddled corpse of her
foster- mother. Nuns took her in, and attempted to
"civilise" her; she is more wolf than girl, walking on

all fours, sniffing the air with her sharp nose. But the nuns finally reject the task, and hand her over to the "bereft and unsanctified household" of the local Duke.

The Duke is sinister and strange; his reflection doesn't appear in a mirror. But Wolf-Alice lives mostly in isolation from him – though thanks to what the nuns have taught her, she is able to sweep up the bones and hair that appear in his chamber. She gets her period and is mystified; but finds rags to soak up the blood. She discovers a mirror, and her reflection; she thinks it is a companion. The return of her period is what gives her an understanding of time. Her body matures; sometimes she puts on the Duke's grandmother's ball dresses and wears them. Once she finds a bridal dress and puts that on – and goes out at night to find a congregation singing in the church.

They have been brought there at night by the husband of a young woman who was the Duke's victim; they aim to lure him out and kill him. They shoot him, but do not kill him – he runs away with Wolf-Alice chasing after him, looking like a bride in her white dress, terrifying the congregation. Back at the castle she tends to the wounded Duke, licking him and healing him with her rough tongue.

What is Carter trying to achieve in *The Bloody Chamber*?

The Bloody Chamber,[*] first published in 1979, is a book of ten tales that are linked by connections of imagery, ideas and theme. While the book is by no means a novel, it has a greater sense of unity than many collections of short stories. And *The Bloody Chamber*, furthermore, does not consist of "stories" – at least not as Carter defined them. In her first collection, *Fireworks*, published three years before, she drew a careful distinction between the story and the tale.

> Formally, the tale differs from the short story in that it makes few pretences at the imitation of life. The tale does not log everyday experience, as the short story does; it interprets everyday experience through a system of imagery derived from subterranean areas behind everyday experience, and therefore the tale cannot betray its readers into a false knowledge of everyday experience. [*Fireworks*, 133]

This description is very useful when it comes to

[*] *The Bloody Chamber* in italics refers to the volume; names of individual stories are not italicised. Page numbers refer to the Vintage edition (see bibliography).

analysing *The Bloody Chamber*. Much modern fiction – certainly fiction that is considered to be "literary" – attempts what Carter calls the imitation of life. Even books such as A. S. Byatt's *Possession* or Ian McEwan's *Atonement* – both of which test the reader's understanding about the "truth" of the stories they are telling by the manner in which they are told – are built from narratives and characters that one might expect to encounter in the world which exists outside books.

Carter's tales in *The Bloody Chamber*, on the other hand, make no attempt to imitate everyday life; and indeed one might say that as the volume progresses they become further and further removed from everyday life. The first, title story – also by far the longest – is the one most superficially rooted in the "real" world. It begins, after all, on a train – our narrator and heroine is steaming through the night to her husband's home. It is set in the past, but it is a recognisable rather than a mythical or generalised past: she rides in a "wagon-lit" (or sleeping compartment) [1] of what is clearly a steam train because of its "great pistons"; her mother's adventurous girlhood was spent in "Indo-China"[1], the French colonial empire in southeast Asia which had its heyday at the end of the 19th century. An ancestor of her husband's knew Catherine de Medici [4]; the Terror of the French Revolution is mentioned [6]; at the opera they hear Wagner's *Tristan und Isolde*

Sarah Patterson in the 1984 film The Company of Wolves, *based on* Angela Carter's *short story.*

[5]. There are guns and telephones and pianos in this story – and yet the events that occur are not the kind of events that occur in the 'real' world.

What does it mean to "interpret everyday experience through a system of imagery derived from subterranean areas behind everyday experience"? If the beginning of this story seems to be realistic, by the time we hear of the Marquis's three late wives, all deceased in mysterious circumstances [4], it is clear that we are moving into the territory of the fabulous. And soon it becomes clear that this territory is literally fabulous, when husband and new bride arrive at his castle.

The faery solitude of the place; with its turrets of misty blue, its courtyard, its spiked gate... cut off by the tide from land for half a day... that castle, at home neither on land nor on the water, a mysterious, amphibious place. [8-9]

That this imaginary castle bears a resemblance to Mont St Michel, an extraordinarily beautiful island and abbey off the coast of Normandy, functions as a kind of bridge – or causeway – between the real and the "faery".

Almost all of the stories in *The Bloody Chamber*, the title story included, address issues of transgression and taboo. Although, in the 21st century, we consider our lives to be much less bound by convention and by etiquette than were the lives of our ancestors, the conventions have only changed (from who you 'friend' on Facebook to who you ask out on a date), they have not disappeared. In *The Bloody Chamber*, the Marquis forbids his bride to enter his "private study" [18] in his absence, a little room at the foot of the west tower of the castle. She transgresses against his interdiction – in part because her husband's great wealth means she is bored and has nothing to do. (She can't even occupy herself unpacking her suitcases; the servants have done it for her [21].) In doing so she makes the ghastly discovery of his three dead wives – and sees the fate which will be in store for her.

Here is the "subterranean area behind everyday experience". The Marquis has wealth and power; his bride is poor, and marries him, it is made clear, to a large degree because of his wealth. When her mother (who had "beggared herself for love" in marrying a soldier) asks her daughter if she is sure she loves her prospective husband, the girl replies: "I am sure I want to marry him" [2]. Her marriage is, therefore, itself a transgression against the convention of love; her husband, undressing her on her wedding night "as if he were stripping the leaves off an artichoke" treats her as an object: she is "aghast to feel myself stirring" [11]. Because of her transgression, desire evokes disgust as well – an uneasy blending confirmed when she discovers his collection of sadistic pornography, and sees an image of a girl, "her cunt a split fig below the great globes of her buttocks on which the knotted tails of the cat were about to descend" [13] – the use of the word "cunt" itself a breaking of a taboo.

In The Courtship of Mr Lyon – as in its source tale, that of Beauty and the Beast – the father transgresses by picking a rose from Mr Lyon's garden [46]; in The Erl-King the girl goes into the forest despite the knowledge that "Erl-King will do you grievous harm" [97]. As in the fairy tales and folklore which lie behind these stories, taboos exist in order that they may be broken, that limits can be tested; these taboos, these limits, are not "real" – but then, finally, no fiction is, no matter how "realistically" it seems to be written. As Carter said in her afterward to *Fireworks*, it is thanks to this very lack of superficial realism that "the tale cannot betray its readers into a false knowledge of everyday experience".

Nevertheless, some critics have questioned the suitability of the fairy tale form as a vehicle for exploring the modern world. According to the great historian and critic of folklore, Jack Zipes, fairy tales "have always been truthful metaphorical reflections of the customs of their times – that is, of the private and public interrelations of people from different social classes seeking power to determine their lives". Like Zipes, Charles Dickens, in the 19th century, believed that fairy tales express fundamental truths about the world. "It would be hard to estimate the amount of gentleness and mercy that has made its way among us through these slight channels," he wrote of the fairy tale form. "Forbearance, courtesy, consideration for the poor and aged, kind treatment of animals, the love of nature, abhorrence of tyranny and brute force – many such good things have been first nourished in the child's heart by this powerful aid".

The influential 20th-century feminist, Andrea Dworkin, however, rejected fairy tales for the same reason Dickens embraced them. She thinks the fairy tale form itself, in its presentation of character and situation (even as re-imagined by

Carter) should be unacceptable to modern women. "Fairy tales are the primary information of the culture. They delineate the roles, interactions, and values which are available to us. They are our childhood models, and their fearful, dreadful content terrorizes us into submission – if we do not become good, then evil will destroy us; if we do not achieve the happy ending, then we will drown in the chaos." For women, fairy tales only offer a damaging, limiting model of behaviour. "There are two definitions of woman. There is the good woman. She is a victim. There is the bad woman. She must be destroyed. The good woman must be possessed. The bad woman must be killed, or punished. Both must be nullified" [Dworkin].

The critic Patricia Duncker feels much the same as Dworkin. While Carter's tales are

JACK ZIPES

Jack Zipes is an academic of Comparative Literature, who has taught and published extensively on the topic of fairy tales, their evolution historically and their social function. Of the fairy tale tradition he has said they "serve a meaningful social function, not just for compensation but for revelation: the worlds projected by the best of our fairy tales reveal the gaps between truth and falsehood in our immediate society". This quote relates closely to Angela Carter's own application of the fairy tale form; her writing constantly plays with the reader's conception of "truth" and "falsehood", the expectations the reader brings to a piece of "fiction", and therefore the social function that this kind of literature has. ∎

supposedly "celebrations of erotic desire", she says, heterosexual feminists "have not yet invented an alternative, anti-sexist language of the erotic. Carter envisages women's sensuality simply as a response to male arousal. She has no conception of women's sexuality as autonomous desire." Writing five years after *The Bloody Chamber* appeared, Duncker took issue with the notion that there is something primal about fairy tales.

> Here, I believe, [Carter] is wrong. The unconscious is not a treasure vault containing visionary revelations about ourselves. It is rather the cesspool of our fears and desires, filled with the common patterns that are also projections of the ways in which we have been taught to perceive the world.

Carter's style is "genuinely original", but Duncker can't get away from the character of the original material.

> The infernal trap inherent in the fairy tale, which fits the form to its purpose, to be the carrier of ideology, proves too complex and pervasive to avoid. Carter is rewriting the tales within the strait-jacket of their original structures. The characters she re-creates must, to some extent, continue to exist as abstractions. Identity continues to be defined by role, so that shifting

the perspective from the impersonal voice to the inner confessional narrative as she does in several of the tales merely explains, amplifies and re-produces rather than alters the original, deeply, rigidly sexist psychology of the erotic.

According to Duncker, Carter's work is still too enmeshed in the male/female, dominant/ submissive hegemony to have truly broken free and into something new.

Other critics disagree. Merja Makinen, writing in *Feminist Review* in 1992, thinks Carter's book is "a book of stories about fairy stories" (as Carter herself said it was), and this ironic stance needs to be acknowledged – it allows the "re-appropriation" of the discourse being critiqued. "I want to argue that Carter's tales do not simply 'rewrite' the old tales by fixing roles of active sexuality for their female protagonists – they 're- write' them by playing with and upon (if not preying upon) the earlier misogynistic version." They are able to do this because of the time when they are written: Carter's readers, in other words, would have been fully aware of a new feminist discourse in literature.

This is true though, as Makinen acknowledges, Carter's text is ambiguous, or, as she puts it, "open-ended". It is just this open-endedness, perhaps, that has created conflict among critics. As Ali Smith has written, while Carter "made the conservative critics angry with what they took as her humourless postmodern political correctness, she made the feminists angry by being far too funny and politically incorrect" [Sage, 5].

Carter herself was always clear about what these tales were *not*: "My intention was not to do 'versions' or, as the American edition of the book said, horribly, 'adult' fairy tales, but to extract the latent content from the traditional stories and use it as the beginnings of new stories". What makes the tales of *The Bloody Chamber* so striking is the way that "traditional" taboos and transgressions are interrogated by the narratives and characters.

The tale of the title story makes explicit the link between sex and death that is only implied in Charles Perrault's *Bluebeard*, or The Robber Bridegroom as told by the Brothers Grimm. Stories of young girls going off to be married must be stories about the discovery of sex: yet in those older tales there is no mention of what lies in store for the new bride. One of the most striking new elements added by Carter is her vibrant depiction of female sexuality and the female body, and the way in which she gives her heroines agency over their own fate. That, in a sense, is what these stories could be said to be "about". In Charles Perrault's *Bluebeard,* the bride is rescued by her brothers – here it is her fearless mother who comes to her rescue, riding up to the castle on a great horse. The mother is a "wild thing... her hat seized by the winds and blown out to sea so that her hair was her white mane, her black lisle legs exposed to the thigh, her skirts tucked round her waist, one hand on the reins of the rearing horse while the other clasped my father's service revolver" [40].

In this one image of the heroine's mother are many transgressions against the cultural conventions of the time – she rides hatless, astride (when women were expected to ride side-saddle) and toting a gun. Like the girl in The Company of Wolves, "she was nobody's meat", that is clear [138].

The Bloody Chamber may therefore be described as a book that plays with convention. It takes the accepted, "traditional" form of the fairy tale and transforms that form into something new. Carter's tales, in their clear-eyed depiction of human sexuality and human agency show the way in which the patriarchal world these characters (both male and female) inhabit attempts to thwart that sexuality and that agency. The tales act almost as lenses through which we can see our own world, and the constraints under which we must operate. There may not be werewolves or vampires in our day-to-day lives: but there are monsters enough, and not just of our imagining.

FIVE FACTS ABOUT
Angela Carter & *The Bloody Chamber*

1.
Angela Carter began to write a sequel to Charlotte Brontë's classic novel *Jane Eyre*, but died before it was completed.

2.
'The Company of Wolves' was adapted into a film in 1984, starring David Warner and Angela Lansbury. Angela Carter co-wrote the screenplay.

3.
The Bloody Chamber was chosen for the 2012 Follio Society/House of Illustration's annual Book Illustration Competition. It was won by Igor Karash.

4.
As a child, Carter was teased at school for being overweight. She later came to battle anorexic in her teenage years.

5.
Carter's novel *Nights At The Circus* won the prestegious James Tait Black Memorial Prize – the world's oldest literary award – in 1984. It was then named the best ever winner of the prize in 2012, which has also recognised work by writers such as EM Forster, Zadie Smith and Graham Greene.

Opposite: Angela Carter, photo by John Mahler in 1988

What kind of world does Carter create in the book?

Angela Carter was born Angela Stalker in Eastbourne, shortly after the outbreak of World War Two. Her father was a journalist and in her early career she worked as a journalist too – and wrote not only novels and stories but journalism and reviews throughout her writing life. She passed the 11-plus and went on to grammar school; she studied English at the University of Bristol, specialising in the literature of the Middle Ages – this would have a lasting effect on her work. She married Paul Carter in 1960 (they divorced in 1972 but she kept his name) and her first novel, *Shadow Dance*, was published in 1966. It was, however, *The Magic Toyshop* (1967) which brought her wider acclaim, winning the John Llewellyn Rhys Memorial Prize. Its story, about a girl's peculiar, damaging awakening into adulthood, foreshadows many of the themes in *The Bloody Chamber*.

In 1969, after separating from her husband, she travelled to Japan, where she lived for two years. She found the depiction of women in Japanese art and culture disturbing; later she would write that in Japan she learnt "what it is to be a woman and became radicalised" [*Nothing Sacred*]. In 1979 – the same year *The Bloody Chamber* appeared –

she also published *The Sadeian Woman*, which looks at the way sex and sexuality are portrayed in modern culture through the lens of the work of the Marquis de Sade, the 18th-century libertine whose pornographic works led to the coining of the term "sadism" – and whose title she gives to the heroine's sinister husband in The Bloody Chamber. What was striking about *The Sadeian Woman* was the way in which Carter gave agency to de Sade's heroines, who are usually seen only as victims. Two years before this, in 1977, Carter published a translation of the French fairy tales of Charles Perrault, several of which are transformed in *The Bloody Chamber*.

By the time *The Bloody Chamber* appeared, then, Carter was already a well-established writer and the collection was widely praised. Ian McEwan called the stories "magnificent set pieces of fastidious sensuality". *The Observer* said that the book "demonstrates Angela Carter's narrative gift at its most mocking and seductive". Jacky Gillott, in *The Times*, wrote:

It has been said that Miss Carter has reworked familiar fairy tales in the light of keener contemporary psychological insight. To have done that alone would have been a witty and scholarly piece of transposition. But she has done far more. She has extended the life and richness of the fable form itself partly through language

that is both pellucid and sensual, but chiefly through imagination of such Ariel reach she can glide from ancient to modern, from darkness to luminosity, from depravity to comedy without any hint of strain and – most valuable of all – without losing the elusive power of the original tales. For every perceptive beam she cast in one corner she replenishes another with riddles...
[January 10, 1980]

In the *Times Literary Suppliment* Susan Kennedy was equally enthusiastic:

> With this collection of stories, ten in all, each a polished artefact, Angela Carter extends her

POSTMODERNISM

The modernist movement, which became prominent in the early 20th century, arose in reaction to traditional forms of art, architecture, literature, etc. Ezra Pound's 1934 injunction – "Make it new!" – sums up the approach, though some of its innovations, like abstract art and the stream-of-consciousness novel, had their origins in the late 19th century. Postmodernism is a term used to describe subsequent changes and tendencies in the arts – changes which have occurred since the late 1940s or early 1950s. Its practitioners deliberately distance themselves from modernism. Postmodernism in literature includes the use of parody or pastiche, an experimental style, magical realist elements and a prevailing tone of irony and knowingness: the writing is usually self-aware and self-referential. ∎

control over an area of the imagination on which she has already left her mark. Her re-telling of European folk and fairy tales has the power not only to cause us to think again, and deeply, about the mythic sources of our common cultural touchstones, but to plunge us into hackle-raising speculation about aspects of our human/animal nature... [These tales work] on our imagination, undermining and reshaping its archetypes. [February 8, 1980]

In thinking about the aims of *The Bloody Chamber*, and addressing how the tales work, it's useful to glance at another writer who influenced Carter: the American writer Edgar Allen Poe, whose mysterious and macabre tales were published in the mid 19th century. She saw his work and her own as part of the "gothic" tradition in literature, which, she wrote, "retains a singular moral function – that of provoking unease" [*Fireworks*, 133]. As Gina Wisker has written, Carter's work, like Poe's, "explores themes of hypocrisy, deceit, duplicity, delusion, incarceration, repression and the explosion of the unfamiliar and the unpleasant from the everyday... she stirs together a wicked (both evil, and celebrated) mix of Gothic horror's terrifying, entrapping paralysis and the energetic agency of the imaginative and actively liberating comic, the carnivalesque" [Wisker, 180].

The stories in *The Bloody Chamber* are not

comfortable to read. They question accepted conventions of behaviour (the perceived passivity of women's sexuality; women's perceived lack of aggressiveness) by painting a compelling, sensual portrait of an alternate world in which those conventions are disrupted. The language is richly descriptive, making it almost impossible not to fall under the spell that Carter is weaving: in the title story the narrator compares her husband's unlined, almost waxy flesh to a lily, a flower closely associated with death – "one of those cobra-headed, funereal lilies whose white sheaths are curled out of a flesh as thick and tensely yielding to the touch as vellum" [3-4]; later, after her wedding night, when the Marquis has left for New York, she lies in their bed and thinks of him: "The perfume of the lilies weighed on my senses; when I thought that, henceforth, I would always share these sheets with a man whose skin, as theirs did, contained that toad-like, clammy hint of moisture, I felt a vague desolation..." She longs for her husband but at the same time "he disgusted me" [19].

The conflict between desire and disgust is what makes the story both interesting and morally complex. Like the whole collection, it acknowledges that its heroines need not reject their desires to be striking, powerful figures – though the desires they experience are often disturbing.

In Carter's tales, desire and morality are both presented as very complex. The narrator of The

Erl-King knows that "Erl-King will do you grievous harm" [97] and yet she seeks him out – and when she find him paints him a strangely domestic setting, almost as if he were a woman. "He is an excellent housewife. His rustic home is spic and span," we are told [99]. And yet it is clear he has power over both the woodland creatures on whom he depends – and over his visitor. "He is the tender butcher who showed me how the price of flesh is love; skin the rabbit, he says! Off come all my clothes" [100]. Desire and danger are deeply intertwined in this tale; at the end of this story it is Erl-King who becomes a victim, his visitor's hands "as gentle as rain" as she strangles him [104]. And what are we to make of the Count in The Snow Child, who calls into being the girl of his dreams – and has sex with her dead body after her death is brought about by his wife, the Countess?

To the critic Merja Makinen, Carter's aims are audacious. "I believe Carter is going some way towards constructing a complex vision of female psycho-sexuality, through her invoking of violence as well as the erotic," she writes. "But that women can be violent as well as active sexually, that women can choose to be perverse, is clearly not something allowed for in the calculations of such readers as [Patricia] Duncker..." Makinen considers Erl-King "a complex rendering of a subjective collusion with objectivity and entrapment within the male gaze". The Snow

Child "presents the unattainability of desire, which will always melt away before possession".

Patricia Duncker is wrong to see Carter as trapped in a traditional view of male/female stereotypes, says Makinen. "Read the beasts as projections of feminine libido, and they become exactly that autonomous desire which the female characters need to recognise and reappropriate as a part of themselves." Margaret Atwood – an accomplished novelist and critic who looked closely at Carter's work – also believes that the stories in *The Bloody Chamber* do not offer a clean division between hunter and hunted. In *The Sadeian Woman*, says Atwood, Carter draws a distinction between "tigers" and "lambs", carnivores and herbivores, "those who are preyed upon and those who do the preying". What Carter seems to be doing in *The Bloody Chamber*, however, is "looking for ways in which the tiger and the lamb, or the tiger and lamb parts of the psyche, can reach some sort of accommodation" [Sage, 134/136]. Certainly, Carter's stories do not pass judgement; unlike in the stories of Charles Perrault, there is no moral here. Instead there are images that haunt us, stay in our minds, cause us to question the judgements we might wish to make. In this context, writes Marina Warner,

Angela Carter made an inspired, marvellous move, for which so many other writers as well as readers will always be indebted to her: she refused to join in rejecting or denouncing fairy tales, but instead embraced the whole stigmatized genre, its stock characters and well-known plots, and with wonderful verve and invention, perverse grace and wicked fun, soaked them in a new fiery liquor that brought them leaping back to life. [Marina Warner, Folio edition of *The Bloody Chamber*]

How radical is *The Bloody Chamber*?

Many of these stories could be described as journeys from innocence to experience. In the title story, the heroine believes that by marrying the Marquis, she and her mother will be released from the bonds of poverty; money will bring happiness. In a sense, then, this story could be said to be as much about finance as it is about sex: can't buy me love, as the saying goes. Carter takes care to describe the Marquis's home, his possessions, in mouth-watering detail, so that the reader is complicit in the narrator's desire for gowns by Worth and a choker made from glittering rubies. It is the poor, blind piano-tuner who will bring the tale's narrator happiness, and although she inherits the Marquis's fortune, she gives most of it away.

The narrator's innocence is also sexual, however, in the traditional (if almost always unspoken) manner of fairy tales. The Marquis is a "satyr" – one of the goat-like, lecherous figures from Greek mythology – who is, the narrator tells us, "captivated [by]... the silent music... of my unknowingness" [16]. When he has sex with her for the first time, a process she describes as being "impaled" [14], he makes explicit what he has taken from her. "'The maid will have changed our sheets already,' he said. 'We do not hang the bloody sheets out of the window to prove to the whole of Brittany you are a virgin, not in these civilized times'" [15-16]. By simply saying this he makes it clear that it would have, of course, been in his power to do so if he so chose; she is a "child" [16], he is the one with absolute control.

Or so he thinks: for even though she is no longer a virgin after their wedding night, her innocence is clearly part of what enables her – along with her heroic mother – to overthrow the Marquis; note that he tells her his first three wives, all of whom met dreadful fates, were not virgins when they came to his bed. ("I should tell you it would have been the first time in all my married lives I could have shown my interested tenants such a flag" [16].)

The narrator of The Tiger's Bride is also a virgin – the Beast wishes to see "the sight of a young lady's skin that no man has seen before"

[68]. It is this that gives her power over the beast, and, in some senses, the power of virginity is an element lifted cleanly from the kind of traditional story of which Andrea Dworkin would so disapprove (and which Dickens, by contrast, would applaud). However, as in so many of these stories, Carter takes the conventional and transforms it, just as her heroines are themselves transformed: in this story it is not the Beast who is altered but the narrator, the Beast's rough tongue licking and licking her to reveal her "beautiful fur" [75].

It is worth remarking, however, that in traditional fairy tales only female virginity is prized; this is another convention Carter upends. The Lady of the House of Love is the story of a beautiful female vampire, "the last bud of the poison tree that springs from the loins of Vlad the Impaler who

TRANSGRESSION

From the Latin *trans* meaning 'across' and 'gressus' from 'gradior' meaning 'to step or walk', it literally means 'to move across' a boundary or line. 'Transgression' is a word that applies generally to the violation of any social or moral boundaries, but also has a specific meaning in the context of art. Transgressive art – that is literature as well as film – painting or any other art form, is characterised by its typically experimental use of forms, and its challenge to orthodox social, moral or political views. In the case of *The Bloody Chamber*, the ten tales might be described as 'transgressive' because of both their content and their form; the way in which they challenge the tradition of fairy tales and what they are about. ∎

37

picnicked on corpses in the forests of Transylvania" [109]. The descriptions of her castle are reminiscent of Dickens's depiction of another isolated, damaged female figure, Miss Havisham from *Great Expectations*: vampire-like Miss Havisham tells Pip that she has "never seen the sun" since before Pip was born; the "rot and fungus everywhere" in Carter's vampire castle recall the decayed state of Miss Havisham's Satis House; like Miss Havisham, the Lady wears a wedding dress; and as Pip and Estella play cards to entertain Miss Havisham, so the Lady of the House of Love turns her Tarot cards.

And as Pip enters Satis House as an innocent boy, so does the young British officer enter Carter's castle, a hearty chap who has decided to take a cycling holiday through "the little known uplands of Romania", otherwise known as Transylvania. Carter says plainly that he "has the special quality of virginity, most and least ambiguous of states: ignorance, yet at the same time, power in potent, and furthermore, unknowingness, which is not the same as ignorance"[112]. It is unusual for a male character's virginity to be so explicitly referred to – especially in the context of the traditional story or fairy tale – and it is a mark of Carter's ability to give her own twist to the tropes of the tradition around which she works that virginity here is as powerful in a man as it in in a woman. At the end of the story – after the Countess cuts herself – it is he who tastes her blood, rather than the other way around [122]. His purity enables this reversal of their roles, and it protects him – although not from the fate which finally awaits him on the battlefields of the First World War.

Carter's bold use of a man's virginity is typical of the boundary-breaking evident throughout this volume. Her work is characterised by its fearlessness, its willingness to shock – and therefore to cause her readers to ask themselves *why they are shocked*. It's too simple to label Carter a "feminist" writer, though of course, at one level, she is one and to some critics, like John Bayley, her ideological feminism was a weakness in her writing; where Margaret Atwood saw a praiseworthy female subversiveness, Bayley – looking over the body of her work not long after she died – opined that she made "imagination itself into the obedient handmaid of ideology", adding: "That would not worry many in the latest generation of critics, who read literature past and present by the light of political correctness. But Carter's new woman combines correctness with being a sort of jolly feminine Tom Jones, what Carmen Callil in a loving obituary has called 'the vulgarian as heroine'". If there is a common factor in the "elusive category of the postmodern novel", says Bayley, "it is political correctness: whatever spirited arabesques and feats of descriptive imagination Carter may perform she always comes to rest in the right ideological position".

Bayley believes that Jane Austen and Virginia Woolf would have greatly admired Carter, "recognized her as one of themselves and been greatly interested in her books, although they might have missed in them the privacy and individuality, the more secret style of independence, which they valued as much as good writing, and which is the supreme gift to us of their novels".

The women in *The Bloody Chamber* are powerful characters, and memorable, even if, in keeping with the tradition of the fairy tale, most of them don't have names and they lack what Bayley calls "the privacy and individuality" of Jane Austen's heroines. In the radical literary tradition of which Carter is a part, however, perhaps the most important influence is not Austen but Charlotte Bronte. "It was Charlotte Brontë who inaugurated with full force the critique of fairy-tale romance in fiction by women for women," says the academic and folklorist Maria Tatar. "The life story of the heroine of *Jane Eyre*, (1847) can be read as a one-woman crusade and act of resistance to the roles modelled for girls and women in fairy tales."

Jane Eyre, like The Bloody Chamber, is, of course, a reworking of Perrault's *Bluebeard*; a young woman comes to live with a man who has a terrible secret hidden in his home. Mr Rochester is released, by Jane, from his secret – his mad first wife hidden in the attic – but only at a terrible price (he survives, but suffers dreadful injuries). In

A scene from Neil Jordan's 1984 film adaptation of 'The Company of Wolves'

Carter's tale, the Marquis cannot survive – but then he is rather less appealing than Mr Rochester.

Less appealing – but not entirely unappealing. The Bloody Chamber is a luxuriant, sensual story, as are all the stories in this collection. Carter's transgressive power lies in her ability to show us how what repels us can also attract us. She does not pass judgment: she describes, and in doing so creates what feels like a brand-new world. "The good-natured power here," Ali Smith has said of this collection, "is in rescuing Red Riding Hood by giving her the fearless naked sensuality that her hood has masked all this time, in letting Beauty also be a Beast, in swapping the so-called reality, by an act of artifice, for a better one" [Sage, 15]. Carter's Red Riding Hood "is a slyly confident adolescent", says John Bayley, "removing her clothes with a sneer to enter the wolf's bed. When he speaks the hallowed formula, 'All the better to eat you with!' 'the girl burst out laughing: she knew she was nobody's meat.' The wolf is not discomfited, but being a politically correct animal at heart he enfolds her in an egalitarian embrace, and they go blissfully to sleep in the eaten-up granny's bed."

These stories are not rich with dialogue: their richness lies in the creation of a lush world that draws the reader in. In The Company of Wolves, a wolf's eyes shining out of the forest are "luminous, terrible sequins" [129]; the girl's red shawl has "the ominous if brilliant look of blood on snow" [133]. When the hunter strips to reveal his true self, "his nipples are ripe and dark as poison fruit" and of course: "His genitals, huge. Ah! huge" [136]. Such fluent, gorgeous – and shocking – descriptions can be found in every tale in this book.

Carter overturns convention most strikingly by revealing how strong our desires – for beauty and for terror – can be. Merja Makinen argues that until we can "take on board the disturbing and often violent elements of female sexuality, we will not be able to decode the full feminist agenda of these fairy tales. We will be unable to recognise the representations of drives so far suppressed by our culture." And Carter herself (talking to Makinen) says that this is precisely the reason why it's important women should write fiction *as women*.

> " ... it is part of the slow process of decolonizing our language and our basic habits of thought. I really do believe this... it has to do with the creation of a means of expression for an infinitely greater variety of experience than has been possible heretofore, to say things for which no language previously existed" [Quoting Carter in *Notes from the Frontline*, in *On Gender and Writing*, editor Michelene Wandor, Pandora, London].

That is the journey from innocence to experience; the dark side of experience is powerful indeed.

FAIRY TALES

Fairy tales in their written form they tend to be a narrative about the fortunes and misfortunes of a hero or heroine who, having experienced various adventures of a more or less supernatural kind, lives happily ever after. Magic, charms, disguise and spells are some of the major ingredients of such stories, which are often subtle in their interpretation of human nature and psychology. ∎

Where does *The Bloody Chamber* fit into literary tradition?

Where does *The Bloody Chamber* belong in what's sometimes called "the fairy tale tradition"? It is important to stress, first, that this is largely an oral tradition. Printed books have only been around for a relatively short time but story-telling is as old as the human race. Indeed the academic John D. Niles refers to *Homo sapiens* as *Homo narrans* – defining us not by our "wisdom" but by our ability to tell stories, and our desire to hear them. It is in the oral tradition, in stories told from mouth to ear, that fairy tales and traditional stories have their roots.

Defining the fairy tale, however, is not simple. Since the time stories told by the fireside have come to be written down, they have been used in a variety of ways. In the early 19th century, the collection of tales from oral tellers was often part of a nationalistic project to promote a "pure" national culture. As Jack Zipes has observed, however, there are no such things as "pure" national folktales or "pure" fairy tales. In fact, both are "very much mixed breeds, and it is the very way that they 'contaminated' each other historically through cross-cultural exchange that has produced fruitful and multiple versions of similar social and personal experiences".

According to Zipes, what we know as the fairy tale, or oral wonder tale, began to take shape in a form we would recognise in the early medieval period; this was when characters and settings and motifs were combined in ways designed to induce awe and wonder in the listener. What does "inducing awe and wonder" really mean, and how do these tales differ from other kinds of fiction? A crucial element is that characters do not demand any explanation for magical events. No scientific explanation is required for the notion that (say) a woodcutter can chop open a wolf and find Red Riding Hood's still-living grandmother tucked safely inside; in the context of the tale, this is simply accepted as fact.

Angela Carter's tales in *The Bloody Chamber* work on the same basis: a child is created from snow; men and beasts are seamlessly blended; a vampire awaits her prey and a cat makes an awfully entertaining narrator. It is important to distinguish this from what is often called "magical realism", when magical elements are woven into otherwise realistic narratives, such as in the work of Salman Rushdie or Gabriel Garcia Márquez. Almost nothing is "realistic" in these stories. The title story is the tale that exists most closely connected to our own, recognisable world; but even in this the "realistic" elements are subservient to the elements of wonder that drive the narrative.

What purpose do these wonder tales serve? The emergence of the literary fairy tales during the latter part of the medieval period, says Zipes, "bears witness to the persistent human quest for an existence without oppression and constraints. It is a utopian quest that we continue to mark down or record through the the metaphors of the fairy tale". It is that quest for an existence without oppression and constraints which brings us back to Angela Carter: for this is not a quest that has gone away, or got any easier, since the latter part of the medieval period. The constraints under which men and women operate have simply changed, they haven't gone away; Carter's tales, broadly speaking, address the "constraint" of the power (im)balance between women and men; and the oppression of women's full sexuality and power.

The Bloody Chamber also fits into the fairy tale tradition because these tales come – in their oral form – from the hearthside. They are thus the provenance of women. As Maria Tatar has written, telling fairy tales has been considered one of the domestic arts ever since Plato, in the Gorgias, discussed the old wives' tales told to children by their nurses – this was in the 4th and 5th century BC. When tales came to be collected in the 19th century, the compilers were nearly always men; the tales themselves, however, were ascribed to women narrators. "The renowned Tales of Mother Goose by Charles Perrault were designated by their author as old wives' tales, 'told by governesses and grandmothers to little children.' And many of the most expansive storytellers consulted by the Grimms were women-family friends or servants who had at their disposal a rich repertoire of folklore" [Tatar, *Classic Fairy Tales*].

There is, of course, no proof that the original tellers of these tales were women; but even before the 19th century rage for collecting tales, women had an important literary role to the play. The term "fairy tale" – *conte de fée* – was coined by a woman, Marie-Catherine Le Jumel de Barneville, Comtesse d'Aulnoy; known from her writing simply as Mme d'Aulnoy.

Born in the middle of the 17th century, she lived a dramatic life; her first book, a novel, was published in 1690 and her first volume of fairy tales in 1697-98. And she was not alone – women writers, during this period in France, produced two-thirds of all the fairy tales which appeared. Why should this be? As Lewis Seifert, an expert in this period, has written, the fairy tale allowed these women to assert their place in society as writers; and, specifically, their own gendered relation to the culture and to the creation of cultural artefacts. "They use the form to create a counter-ideology in which women assert their own abilities and desires to participate in cultural and, especially, literary production" [Seifert, in *TGFFT*, 932]. Angela Carter, who had translated the tales of Charles

Perrault, and knew a great deal about French literary tradition, would have seen herself as firmly aligned with women such as Mme d'Aulnoy.

What is most striking about the fairy tale is its flexibility: the broad strokes of its stock characters and magical events allow for constant reinterpretation and re-evaluation; *The Bloody Chamber* is one link in a fascinating and flexible chain – and one that continues to be forged. From books such as Neil Gaiman's *Coraline* (2002), to Hollywood efforts such as *Enchanted* (2007) or *Snow White and the Huntsman* (2012), the fairy tale remains a vibrant present in our cultural heritage.

A SHORT CHRONOLOGY

1940 May 7 Angela Carter born Angela Olive Stalker in Eastborne

1962 Carter reads English at Bristol University, specialising in Medieval Literature

1967 *The Magic Toyshop* published

1969 *Several Perceptions* wins the Somerset Maugham Award, the same year *Heroes and Villains* is published

1974 *Fireworks: Nine Profane Pieces*

1977 *The Passion of New Eve*

19779 *The Bloody Chamber*

1977 Carter's only child, Alex, is born

1984 *Nights At The Circus* wins the James Tait Black Memorial Prize for literature

1992 February 16 Carter dies of lung cancer aged 52, just a year after being diagnosed

2012 Angela Carter named best ever winner of the James Tait Black Memorial Prize

FURTHER READING

Other works by Angela Carter:

Angela Carter, *Fireworks: Nine Profane Pieces*, London, Quartet Books, 1976

Angela Carter, T*he Bloody Chamber*, with an introduction by Marina Warner, London, Folio Society, 2012

Angela Carter, *The Bloody Chamber*, with an introduction by Helen Simpson, London, Vintage, 2006) NB: all page references are to this edition

Angela Carter, *Nothing Sacred: Selected Writings by Angela Carter*, London, Virago, 1982

Useful criticism:

Margaret Atwood, "Running with the Tigers", *Flesh and the Mirror: Essays on the ART of Angela Carter*, London, Virago, 1994, pp.117-135

John Bayley, "Fighting for the Crown", *New York Review of Books*, 23 April 1992

BBC, A video excerpt from the BBC FOUR documentary 'Introducing Angela Carter' (including interviews with the author)

Susannah Clapp, *A Card from Angela Carter*, London, Bloomsbury, 2012

Susannah Clapp, An audio discussion of Angela Carter's writing, including a reading of one of the tales, 'The Tiger's Bride', from BBC Radio 4

Patricia Duncker, "Re-Imagining the Fairy Tales: Angela Carter's Bloody Chambers", *Literature and History: A Journal of the Humanities*, 10.1, Spring 1984

Andrea Dworkin, *Woman Hating*, New York, Penguin, 1974

Merja Makinen, "Angela Carter's The Bloody Chamber and the Decolonization of Feminine Sexuality", *Feminist Review*, No. 42, Autumn 1992, pp. 2-15

Lorna Sage (ed.), *Flesh and the Mirror: Essays on the Art of Angela Carter*, London, Virago, 2007

Lewis Seifert, "The Marvellous in Context: The Place of the Contes de Fées in Late 17th-Century France", in J. Zipes (ed.) *The Great Fairy Tale Tradition from Straparola and Basile to the Brothers Grimm*, 2001, p.913

Helen Simpson, "Femme fatale", A reappraisal of *The Bloody Chamber* in *The Guardian*, 14 June 2006

Maria Tatar (ed.), *The Classic Fairy Tales*, New York, W. W. Norton, 1999

Marina Warner, discusses *The Bloody Chamber* in a series of videos for The Folio Society (further video links along the left margin on the link page)

Marina Warner, chapter from *Angela Carter and the Fairy Tale*

Marina Warner, "Chamber of Secrets: The Sorcery of Angela Carter", *The Paris Review*, 17 October 2012

Marina Warner, "Marina Warner on why Angela Carter's *The Bloody Chamber* still bites", *The Scotsman*, excerpt from Warner's introduction to the Folio Society's edition.

Jack Zipes, A video lecture on 'Utopian Tendencies of Oddly Modern Fairy Tales'

Jack Zipes (ed.), *The Great Fairy Tale Tradition from Straparola and Basile to the Brothers Grimm*, New York, W. W. Norton, 2001

Jack Zipes, "Cross-Cultural Connections and the Contamination of the Classical Fairy Tale", in J. Zipes (ed.) *The Great Fairy Tale Tradition from Straparola and Basile to the Brothers Grimm*, 2001, pp.845-869

Jack Zipes, "A short interview with Jack Zipes", Biting Dog Press, April 2002

Notes

Notes

First published in 2016 by
Connell Guides
Artist House
35 Little Russell Street
London WC1A 2HH

10 9 8 7 6 5 4 3 2 1

Picture credits:
p.17 © REX Features/ITV/Shutterstock
p.27 © Getty Images/John Muhler
p.41 © REX Features/ ITV/Shutterstock

A CIP catalogue record for this book is available from the British Library.
ISBN 978-1-911187-01-1

Design © Nathan Burton
Written by Erica Wagner
Assistant Editor and typeset by:
Paul Woodward and Holly Bruce

Printed in Great Britain

www.connellguides.com